20/20 Prudent Leadership: Who Am I?

By LauraAnn Migliore, Ph.D. & Erik Bean, Ed.D.

Illustrations by Gail Gorske

20/20 Prudent Leadership: Who Am I?

By LauraAnn Migliore, Ph.D. & Erik Bean, Ed.D.

Illustrations by Gail Gorske

ISBN: 978-1-7347801-2-3

For more information on this book series visit:
PrudentLeadership.com

DEDICATION

We dedicate this book series to all those who value personal freedom to self-govern, self-help, and self-lead in the practical application of doing what they can, with what they have, and where they are at.

Contents

FOREWORD Who Am I? is the subject of Book 3 in our 9-book series. We chose May 22nd for this particular installment as it corresponds to a Theodore Roosevelt milestone that celebrates a reflection of legislation, a gift of beauty and tranquility for the public to enjoy for decades to come, the date upon which he signed to preserve the 6th United States National Park, Crater Lake, located in Oregon. "As in water face reflects face, so a person's heart reveals the person" (Proverbs 27:19). In this edition we will spend much time reflecting, analyzing a question that individuals have asked for centuries, *Who Am I?* A simple question, yet one that also has perplexed so many for it constantly impinges on our values and the authenticity shaped by our geographical location, our faith, religion, gender, race, and heritage. A simple question yet so challenging to sum up and answer for our characterization of who we are can change on a day-to-day basis. While we may have primary beliefs, which remain firmly in place, other beliefs can change and fluctuate dramatically over time. Such beliefs can ebb and flow built upon personal as well as community events, the likes of which continue to change in the midst of the COVID-19 pandemic, not to mention the various risks we take during more stable times.

Whoever you are, whoever you may turn out to be, also is shaped by your accomplishments, your profession, your livelihood, and how others might categorize you. But it is your actions through the premise of Book 2 — conversation, conduct, and character bearing prudence, that is the authenticity to allow you and those around you to assess who you are. By examining a swath of history in Christianity, Judaism, and from the Islamic perspectives, we will lay the framework of how others have pondered this question. Then we will try to hit the ball out of the park by examining the legendary baseball powerhouse Babe Ruth as well as a lesser known player Moe Berg who not only played in the major leagues, but was an attorney and United States spy during World War II. How did the public categorize who they were? How might they have seen themselves? All the while, we will ask you to continue to reflect on the values we started to discuss in Book 1 and we will help you visualize who you are. But take note. Labels can harm the psyche and are only a snapshot in time, of any perspective that comprises your consciousness. So, suit up. Get your glove, cap, and adorn your COVID mask if you think it can help you divulge who you are. For after this installment we are prudently preparing you to be *Programmed for Excellence* in Book 4.

Our world has changed forever. The future is uncertain. But your physical, spiritual, and mental health is of utmost importance particularly with regard to your ability to self-lead and lead those who you represent. How you react to it is your choice. Like Theodore Roosevelt, your legacy also will sum up who you are, what you have done, your public role and those private moments with family and friends that can never be quite measured. With much admiration for your continued success,

LauraAnn Migliore, Ph.D. and Erik Bean, Ed.D.

LauraAnn Migliore   *Erik Bean*

May 22, 2020

1. Introduction

One of the most perplexing questions of life consists of three simple words: *Who Am I?* There are so many identities and roles picked up as we go through life's journey – mother, father, husband, wife, baseball player, software developer, therapist, executive, professor, entrepreneur, engineer, to name a few. The list of identities can be quite lengthy. However, the truth is that whatever you believe yourself to be is predicated on something else. Therefore, it is important to differentiate true self from an identity that merely describes a role we play when certain conditions are present. For example, you are a mother or father because you have a child; you are a husband because you have a wife and vice versa; you are a baseball player because you play ball; you are an engineer because you learned the disciplines of engineering, etc.

Identities exist because they depend on something else to be present. When that something else is no longer present, the identity gets deactivated. Take for example, baseball legend Babe Ruth (1895–1948). From a young age, his life was focused on playing baseball. He learned every position, perfected his talent, and went on to have an amazing career in Major League Baseball – becoming a true icon in American history and hero to many. Baseball was the epicenter of his life and defined who he was. When he retired, he went on to do good helping others via works of charity, but soon after discovered he was stricken with cancer and died 53-years young.

The mystery behind his private life and what his conversation and conduct revealed about his values and beliefs varies by interpretation of those who knew him best. According to the Society of American Baseball Research, SABR (2020), Babe Ruth had a deep desire to manage a baseball team but for several reasons he did not, such as different perspectives in prudent decision-making, personal disputes with others, and conflicting goals with team owners. For example, he thought he could just move up and not pay his dues because he was Babe Ruth. According to Schwartz (n.d.), Jacob Ruppert, Yankees owner, allegedly told Ruth, "'Manage the Yankees? You can't even manage yourself!'" (para 27).

Another intriguing baseball example is based on a true story of Morris (Moe) Berg (1902 – 1972), who was a catcher in Major League Baseball and blessed with intellect – a graduate of Princeton University and speaker of seven languages (Acocella, n.d.). Moe's love of the game motivated his career choice in professional baseball. However, his father, Bernard Berg, viewed it as a waste of intellect and could not celebrate his son's enthusiasm or appreciate his stories of travel and social hobnobbing that came along with having a professional baseball career.

The unwillingness or inability to see things differently caused contention between father and son. After Moe's father died, the serendipity of life connects Moe to the United States Office of Strategic Services (OSS), predecessor of the Central Intelligence Agency (CIA), where he became a paramilitary officer involved in various operations in Europe (CIA, 2013) and was able to apply his intellect in meaningful ways leveraging his baseball fame.

For example, Berg's baseball connection to U.S. government intelligence began with his membership on the All-Star team with Babe Ruth, Lou Gehrig and other great American ballplayers traveling to Japan in mid-1930s to play ball. According to Acocella (n.d.), his later years were filled with financial struggles living with family and friends, and although he agreed to write a book about his life experiences, the editor botched communications assuming he was signing a contract with Moe of The Three Stooges. This blunder collapsed the book project. The many aspects of Moe's personal and professional life are a mystery as to who he really was. Nevertheless, his life story demonstrates diversity of many levels to remind us what you see on the outside is not always what is going on inside a person's heart and mind and the struggles they deal with on a daily basis.

When Berg traveled with Ruth, Gehrig, and other baseball greats for an All-Star game in Japan in the 1930s, he took advantage of his location for his spy work. Using his communication skills in Japanese, Berg was able to access one of the tallest buildings in Tokyo, all the way to the rooftop and with his movie camera, filmed the capital city's shipyards. Berg's film was then later used by the U.S. to plan its bombing raids over Tokyo during World War II (CIA, 2013).

The answer to the question, "Who Am I" is complex. Our lives are interlaced with people, places, and circumstances that together create spaces where we have no knowledge of self. The way we see ourselves is not always the way others see us. For instance, we may see ourselves as confident and others see us as proud and arrogant. Also, our interests may change over time and we wonder why the change; what's going on to motivate us to do something else; we may subconsciously say, why do I feel like I'm struggling when in times past it was easy, etc.

Developing the habit of self-reflection is important to renew mind and overall mental health. Returning to focus on a centered point of being can also reaffirm self-knowledge and personal epistemological understanding – that is, one's own individual truth to answer the mysterious question of "Who Am I?"

Epistemology is the study of knowledge, justification, and rationality of belief (Stanford Encyclopedia of Philosophy, 2020). When we refer to personal epistemological understanding, it means addressing other complicated questions like "How do I know that I know?" or "What makes my beliefs justified" and "Are my assumptions of rationale accurate to support my opinions and beliefs?" As you can see, these questions are part of the multilayers of inquiry supporting the real question of "Who Am I?"

One famous historical example of self-identity is recorded in the Bible, Gospel of Matthew, Chapter 16 (verses 13-20) when Jesus asks his disciples, "Who do men say that I, the Son of Man am?"

Their responses included, "Some say John the Baptist, some Elijah, and others Jeremiah or one of the prophets."

Then Jesus said to them, "But who do you say that I am?"

Simon Peter answered and said, "You are the Christ, the Son of the living God."

Jesus answered and said to him, "Blessed are you Simon Bar-Jonah, for flesh and blood has not revealed this to you, but My Father who is in heaven. And I also say to you that you are Peter, and on this rock, I will build My Church, and the gates of Hades shall not prevail against it. And I will give you the keys of the kingdom of heaven, and whatever you bind on earth will be bound in heaven, and whatever you loose on earth will be loosed in heaven." Then Jesus commanded his disciples that they should tell no one that He was Jesus the Christ.

According to the Judeo-Christian perspective, the mystery of God is the mystery of you if you choose to believe what the Bible or Torah say as recorded in the Book of Genesis, Chapter 1 (verses 26-28). Please note that a common Jewish approach in communications is not to write out the full name of *G-d*. However, for ease of readability to the non-Jewish believer, we have spelled out the name of God as written in the Bible:

Then God said, "Let Us make man in Our image, according to Our likeness; let them have dominion over the fish of the sea, over the birds of the air, and over the cattle, over all the earth and over every creeping thing that creeps on the earth." So, God created man in His own image; in the image of God He created him; male and female; He created them. Then God blessed them, and God said to them, "Be fruitful and multiply; fill the earth and subdue it; have dominion over the fish of the sea, over the birds of the air, and over every living thing that moves on the earth" (Genesis 1:26-28). This heavenly mandate implies a command to take dominion over the earth and be a leader of self with values and beliefs rooted in personal freedom. Also, to accept responsibility of caring for the earth and applying good stewardship to tend and keep it (Genesis 2:15).

2. Christian Vs. Jewish Vs. Islamic Perspective: Who Am I?

Looking back to ancient Greece, Aristotle defined people as rational human beings. From the earliest Christian perspective of God creating man/woman in his own image (Genesis 1:27) our ability to think and reason comprises the human experience that ponders, Who Am I? The answer is we are the substance created in "'the image of God'" (Chong, 2004, para 15). But when asking the question, Who Am I, we are consciously applying a label – mother, father, dancer, musician, etc.

According to the Jewish perspective, we can further think of ourselves in many ways, but no single personality trait or perspective necessarily defines who you are (Allouche, 2018). People who suffer from psychological disorders typically identify themselves with such a mental illness label. For example, *I am bipolar, I am attention deficit, or I am a meshugana* (Yiddish for crazy). Why not say, *I have* instead of *I am*? *I am* is so definitive. Rabbi Allouche says Moses had spoken in the same manner identifying himself as a stutterer and unqualified for the job God was appointing him to deliver Israel from Pharaoh. Nevertheless, God ignores Moses' perspective and asks him to assume the leadership role and not be limited by his imperfection.

The Islamic perspective maintains that our conduct comprises the lion's share of who we are. The Christian and Jewish perspectives do not necessarily disagree. In this Islamic Unity Society perspective, a British Islam voice, conduct is central to the defining question of Who Am I. "O Mankind! Lo! We have created you male and female, and have made you nations and tribes that ye may know one another. Lo! The noblest of you, in the sight of Allah, is the best in conduct. Lo! Allah is knower, aware" – Holy Quran 49:13 (as cited in Voice of Unity, 2015, para 3).

Enter the Prudent Adam, our character guiding us to rationale thinking based on our values. Prudent Adam would agree that like Theodore Roosevelt would say, how we behave, comprises the bulk of our character. Thus, the Christian, Jewish, and Islamic perspectives provide a platform for discovery, one based on the authenticity of our actions that we discussed in Book 2: Conversation, Conduct, Character, and COVID-19. Our very being and how people view us is a Venn intersection of the first three Cs!

We added COVID-19 in Booklet 2 since its ramifications, like all aspects of life, have been forever changed. That said, who you are is not represented by a single thought or one or two characterizations. Rather who you are is comprised of millions upon millions of atomic actions and the amount of cognitive dissonance you are willing to endure. See Book 1 for the introductory cognitive dissonance anecdote.

The mystery of you is documented throughout the Bible and therefore a highly recommended reading, because it is one of the oldest books in the history of the world. For example, King David in Psalms 82 verses 6-7 writes that God says, "You are gods (with a small "g") and all of you are children of the Most High, but you shall die like men and fall like one of the princes."

Another example is the Epistle of Paul, the Apostle to the Colossians (verses 24-29), where Paul describes the mystery among the Gentiles (non-Jewish), as "Christ in you, the hope of glory" (Colossians 1:27).

King Solomon (son of King David) wrote, "It is the glory of God to conceal a matter; but the glory of kings is to search out a matter" (Proverbs 25:2). Your adventure of self-discovery is to search out and come to know personal authenticity with epistemological understanding.

Carpe diem (Latin for seize the day). Today is the day to seize adventure in self-discovery. If you do not know who you are, you can go through life pursuing new identities that pull you away from your true self causing pain and heartache. Consider the life of Brad Cohen, a man who learned how to overcome incredible obstacles living with Tourette Syndrome in his pursuit of becoming a teacher. Tourette Syndrome is a Tic Disorder expressed involuntary with repetitive movements and vocalizations (Tourette Association of America, n.d.). Cohen was misunderstood by many including those close to him and experienced bullying and rejection, including 24 job interviews for a teacher's position until one principal was willing to give him a chance. Brad attributes Tourette Syndrome to making him become the teacher he never had and has written a book, turned movie, "Front of the Class"(2008). Who Am I? Brad could have settled for I Am Tourette Syndrome. Instead he overcame and possessed a lifestyle of success teaching, writing, and speaking inspiring others to do the same.

26th U.S. President Theodore Roosevelt

The amazing life story of Theodore Roosevelt (TR) is captured in many books, movies, and documentaries, which reveal the multifaceted life of a tenacious man, who always pushed himself to do what others said could not be done. TR lived the strenuous life overcoming his own personal battle with asthma and related physical ailments. The outdoors represented a place for TR to prove himself from cowboying in the Dakotas to big game hunting in the African Safari. His love of the environment was demonstrated during his presidency signing into legislation many national parks and bird reservations. For example, Crater Lake – Oregon became the 6th National Park on May 22, 1902 and it reflects pristine beauty with an intense blue color surrounded by cliffs and fed entirely by rain and snow. Its depth is 1,943 feet making it one of the deepest lakes in the United States (NPS, 2020).

Where once stood a 12,000-foot volcano is now collapsed and dormant covered reflective body of water called Crater Lake. The beauty of which Greek god Narcissus would be so enamored with his own reflection he could drown trying to capture it! "Who Am I? Who Am I?" Narcissus asks.

Greek mythology says Narcissus became stuck and unable to pull himself away from the beauty of his own image and died at the place of his personal bondage of self-addiction; but there the Daffodil flower bloomed and his beauty was transformed into this amazing flower. Then again, perhaps Narcissus had some connection with the "Old Man of the Lake," an ancient hemlock tree that floats upright blown by the winds and not rocked by the waves (Grange, 2011). The stump is a phenomenon of physics floating four feet above the water and 30 feet deep underneath. Strange stories have also been reported of eerie occurrences in the night at Crater Lake and around the uninhabited Wizard Island, a cone-shaped structure in the lake, which are the remains of the dormant volcano.

Lessons to be gleaned from volcanic disruptions like Crater Lake and a self-addiction that entraps: Out of chaos and destruction can come order and beauty. Keep a long-term perspective that things will get better. *God makes everything beautiful in its time* (Ecclesiastes 3:11)

To know you are addicted occurs when you try to stop. Ask for help if you cannot stop and be resolute to break the power of repeating the same bad habit. *If you find honey, EAT just ENOUGH – TOO much of it, and you will vomit.* (Proverbs 25:16)

As a dog returns to his own vomit, so a fool repeats his folly (Proverbs 26:11)

Self-refection is good to learn and lead better. Be kind to self. Forgive self and adopt the attitude of continuous improvement to become the best version of you.

As in water face reflects face, so a man's heart reveals the man (Proverbs 27:19)

Be sure to stay tuned for the release of Book 6 on September 14, the date in 1901 when Theodore Roosevelt became the 26th U.S. president. We are devoting that entire edition to the life of TR and his incredible prudent self-leadership discipline!

3. Hiding Places of Self

Addictions, whatever they may be – food, drugs, alcohol, sex, etc. – are places of escape for pleasure and relief of pain. It is easy to become addicted and hard to break the stronghold of addiction. So, what are the odds that a crack addict would turn successful CEO? Mike Lindell is a shining star example of one who did just that. He beat the odds and shared his incredible success story from drug addiction to visionary leader of the My Pillow company helping millions of people get a better night's sleep. Lindell is seen frequently on television commercials and wrote a book sharing his life story and personal struggle with addiction and attributes his amazing transformation to faith in God. His persistence to overcome was focused on purpose to achieve the dream God gave him for My Pillow and to inspire hope for others who struggle with addictions. His transformative moment happened when he decided he did not want to be addicted anymore and prayed to God to take away his desire for drugs and alcohol (Lindell, 2019). It happened just as he asked because his inner man agreed with the words he spoke to God. When you agree with God, miracles can happen. Walking with God in agreement is a wonderful thing!

Can two walk together, unless they are agreed? (Amos 3:3)

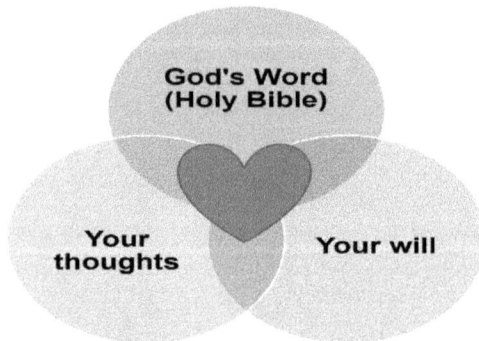

The power of agreement within self is a force to propel you forward to achieve goals and fulfill purpose, which makes life meaningful. Lindell (2019) shared how he could feel his desire for drugs and alcohol was gone when he had that synchronized moment within himself to say, *no more,* and then asked for God's help.

Through one may be overpowered by another, two can withstand him, and a threefold cord is not quickly broken (Ecclesiastes 4:12).

Lindell (2019) describes the miracle as a transformative feeling on the inside, described as a peace he never felt before and a feeling of calm within. In his book, he shares a scenario meeting with potential investors to fund his vision for making My Pillow profitable and described how in the past, he would never have faced the situation without cocaine. That day was different and although he was nervous, he felt usually confident. His elevator pitch of how he could turn a $30,000 cash investment from them into $40,000 return within three months was risky from an investor's point of view, but his transparency about his crack addition and his personal resolve to achieve the goal and turn My Pillow into a profitable company was heard by the investors as authentic and interpreted favorably. They gave him the cash without a formal contract, just an I.O.U and the rest is history about an amazing comeback from addict to successful CEO!

In Book 2, *Conversation, Conduct, Character, & COVID-19* we discussed the power of words and how they influence what you do and included template tools to help identify areas for improvement. These template tools are simple to use and effective when you invite a trusted friend, co-worker, boss, or loved one to provide feedback on the areas identified. We also shared the analogy of the Prudence Atom in Book 1, *20/20 Prudent Leadership: Your Values*, and discussed cognitive dissonance; that uncomfortable feeling when confronted with a situation that conflicts with your values and beliefs. Just like when an atom has more or fewer electrons than protons, the nucleus would have either an overall negative or positive charge – analogy of the Prudence Atom. This out-of-balance condition of an atom is called an ion or free radical and likewise creates a lack of consistency between values and beliefs (protons & neutrons in the nucleus) and emotions, thoughts, and behaviors (electrons).

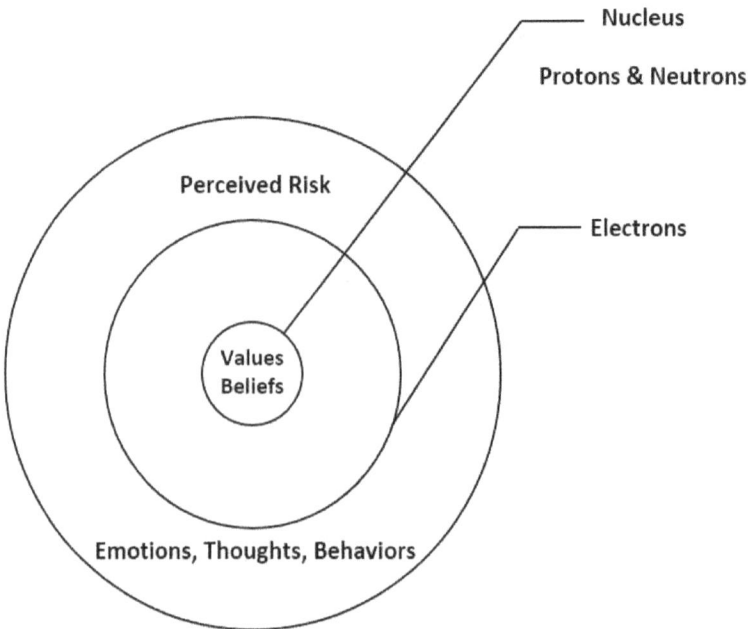

Nucleus

Protons & Neutrons

Perceived Risk

Electrons

Values Beliefs

Emotions, Thoughts, Behaviors

A key lesson to be gleaned from the Lindell story is the **power of internal agreement** of body, mind/spirit, heart/soul. In physics there is a phenomenon of thermodynamics called the **triple point**, which occurs when a substance has temperature and pressure equal at each of the three phases: gas, liquid, and solid (Engineering Insider, 2018). When there is an intersection of equal temperature and pressure at all three phases, the process of sublimation occurs at the molecular level to transition a physical change of state from solid to gas, which bypasses the liquid state. For example, you may have noticed that on a cold sunny day when large piles of snow are pushed onto the edges of roads or parking lots, the snow looks like it is steaming – that is a sign of sublimation when the snow goes directly from solid state to a gas state bypassing the liquid/water state. As an analogy of this triple point phenomenon, the power of agreement of personal will is like the process of sublimation where the inner man (Lindell) came into agreement (mind/spirit and heart/soul) with the words he spoke to God asking that his desire for drugs and alcohol be taken away.

Just like the endothermic (energy) process of sublimation absorbs heat from the temperature and pressure below a substance's triple point – a metaphor likened to God answering Lindell's prayer to cause change to happen without a liquid meltdown. Interesting too is that chemical reactions are not sublimation. In other words, drugs and alcohol are mind-altering substances and only provide temporary satisfaction, not a lasting change.

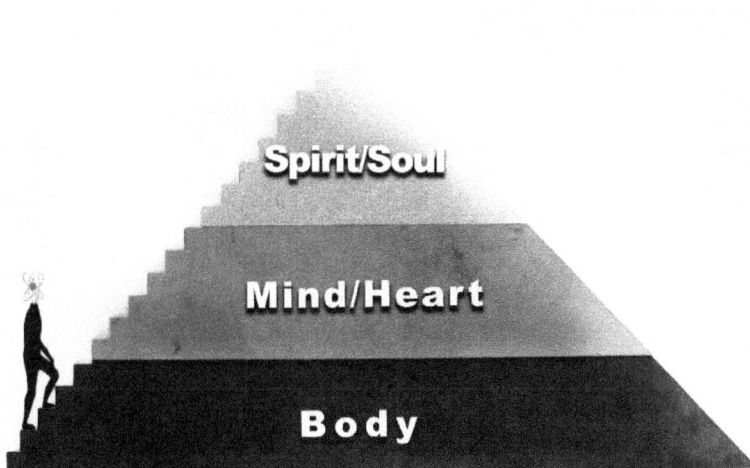

4. The Power of Internal Agreement

There is another unusual life story of a fictional character, named Dorian Gray, that portrays a real person who lived a hedonistic lifestyle during the late 1890's in London, England. However, this story depicts a tragic outcome of cognitive dissonance that creates a pseudo change and hides the true self / authenticity of Dorian Gray. There are several movies and books on the story of Dorian Gray. The story is about a young man who makes a deal with the devil, selling his soul by coming into agreement with a self-portrait painting to preserve his youthful beauty in his physical body and appearance while the self-portrait takes on the ravages of his lifestyle and passage of time. He hides the self-portrait because it reveals his true self – battered and abused, sick and decrepitate from his life of sin, deceit, greed, and vanity.

When Dorain looks in the mirror, he sees his beautiful, handsome, and youthful self and that is also what he portrays to others to see. However, when Dorian looks at the self-portrait painting that he hides from others, he sees his true self, an ugly person. Because, he does not change his values and beliefs, his emotions, thoughts, and behaviors continue to take on the risks of his hedonistic lifestyle. Dorian's prudence is another's provocation – a repelling force of discourse. In Book 1, *Your Values*, we discussed the internal power of values and beliefs and now we connect it to program either a healthy or unhealthy mind to answer the question, *Who Am I?* Enter Dissociative Identity Disorder (DID).

Dissociative Identity Disorder (DID)

There is a fairly new psychological illness called, Dissociative Identity

Disorder (DID), which is a severe form of dissociation in the mental process of a person's thoughts, emotions, memories, behaviors, and overall identify of who one is (WebMD, 2020).

The theory supporting DID intersects a combination of factors that may include a traumatic event or repeated abuse experienced by the person with the disorder. However, it may also be linked to natural disorders of genes, and/or other anomalies of brain conditions not fully understood or diagnosable at the present time. The dissociation occurs where the person cuts himself/herself off from the situation or experience that is too painful to assimilate with his/her conscious self. The process of dissociation can create multiple personalities or a split within one identity of self (Laddis, et.al., 2017). Those at risk for DID include children in early years of development (usually before age of 6) when emotional neglect or abuse can interfere with personality formation.

Studies show children may become dissociative when parents or caregivers are perceived as frightening and unpredictable to the child. Not everyone will experience DID the same way; the dissociation may interfere with identities (imaginary people, animals, extraterrestrials, etc.) having their own age, gender, or race/ethnicity. Each personality is known to control the individuals' emotions, thoughts, and behaviors and the switching process between personalities can vary in time from seconds to minutes to days. These altered states of identity have been described as a feeling of being hijacked in one's own body; like being a passenger in their body with the host personality driving them to do and say things.

People who suffer from DID believe they have no choice in the words they say and actions they do. These fragmented states of identity are not fully mature personalities and represent a disjointed sense of identity. The person suffering from DID can experience distortions in time, space, and perception – a twilight zone experience. The medical treatment for DID typically includes prescription medications, psychotherapy, and hypnosis.

According to Korzekwa, et.al. (2009), people with DID have spent many years in the mental health system prior to receiving an accurate diagnosis. The reason for the lengthy time to diagnosis involves coexisting diagnoses of borderline disorders, depression, or other types of personality disorders like Narcissistic Personality Disorder (NPD). NPD is a disorder where the person has an exaggerated sense of self-importance and entitlement and little to no tolerance towards others' feelings, perspectives, or contributions. NPD is difficult to diagnose (Caligor & Stern, 2020). NPD can look like inflated ego/pride with insatiable taking and little to no giving / reciprocity unless the giving will get them what they want.

One such extreme example comes from the Bible in the Book of Daniel. The Babylonian King Nebuchadnezzar suffered from a mental illness and lived isolated for seven years until he came to acknowledge the ultimate power of one God. The Bible describes Nebuchadnezzar as a dehumanized being, eating grass like a bovine and growing hair like an eagle and nails like a bird (Daniel 4: 25-33). Nebuchadnezzar was an arrogant ruler who disregarded any supreme power except himself. According to famed psychiatrist Carl Jung (1875 – 1961), Nebuchadnezzar was an arrogant ruler who developed psychosis after dreaming of himself (as a tree being cut down) and interpreted as a necessary process for him to achieve internal wholeness.

Another extreme example that ended tragically is the mysterious case of Annaliese Michel (1952 - 1976), a true story of a young German woman who was subjected to Catholic exorcism rites during the year before she died. Her story is also depicted in the movie, "Exorcism of Emily Rose" (2005) along with the usual added embellishments of Hollywood creativity to make the content engaging to watch – suspenseful and scary.

Annaliese was diagnosed with temporal lobe epilepsy, a seizure that occurs from the temporal lobe of the brain and is usually preceded by an aura or unusual sensations of sights, smells, tastes, or a feeling of emotional heaviness (Paoletti, 2017; Cleveland Clinic, 2020). However, the case of Annaliese Michel is complicated with strong religious beliefs instilled from her childhood (Time Magazine, 1976). Her parents and those close to her and the case all believed she was possessed by demons.

Anneliese also believed she was possessed by demons and she was willing to serve as the propitiation of sins for her parents, apostate priests, and others. From the information published, it appears the extreme religious interpretation applied by Anneliese reflects a religious teaching not aligned with scriptures of only Jesus being capable of paying the price for sins. Perhaps the Catholic doctrine that was taught to Anneliese misinformed or caused her misunderstanding of scripture and its application. Nevertheless, the lack of basic life support in medical care such as intravenous feeding seems to provide rational evidence of neglect and abuse in the mysterious case of Anneliese Michel, who died a tortuous death of starvation – only 68 pounds, emaciated and dehydrated (Barclay, 2011).

According to Paoletti (2017), two Catholic priests were found guilty according to German law of her death and sentenced to prison. However, the sentence was later changed to three-month's probation. Anneliese's parents were not further charged based on premise they had suffered enough given the gory details of the case. Whether or not this case is one of demonic possession or mental illness, the strong beliefs of Anneliese and her parents and the priests did not accommodate basic medical life support and she died. The Catholic rites of exorcism failed to bring deliverance as believed possible. *Who was Annaliese?*

People die for lack of knowledge. Within Christianity there are also different understandings of who Jesus is. According to the Bible-believing Christian perspective, Jesus is the propitiation of sins (1 John 2:2). However, the Bible is subject to many interpretations of belief and in Anneliese's case, the evidence indicates she believed serving a greater call in life to suffer for others and she died for her cause.

My people are destroyed for lack of knowledge……(Hosea 4:6).

And He [Jesus]Himself is the propitiation for our sins, and not for ours only but also for the whole world (1 John 2: 2).

Faith or Fear in Self-Discovery

When people search for meaning, as we all do, they can often be torn between faith and fear. Their values and the prudence of their conduct can also fluctuate and reduce authenticity. For most people, they accept the faith they were born into, but others change faiths and pursue a path to self-actualization, which can lead some to discover who they are much later in life. Some people also identify who they are based on milestones and deadlines for meeting these milestones shaped by their belief system. For example, graduate from college by 22; get a job that supports a livelihood; get married by 28 and have kids by 33, retire by 65, etc. However, if they do not achieve a milestone by a certain age, they may interpret that as failure. Prudent Adams says, "stop that stinking thinking and reframe your perspective."

While timelines are important, never underestimate the power within to bloom where you are planted and apply faith to believe that with God, all things are possible! Like Lindell's (2019) amazing transformation story; he came into agreement within himself and with God to overcome the things that were holding him back. That comfort, confidence, and personal freedom to just be you, has no time line other than the immediacy of the responsibilities we all possess, paying our bills, feeding ourselves and our loved ones, abiding by the laws in our community, etc.

The internal power of values and beliefs will drive thoughts, emotions, and behaviors as shown in the Nucleus of the Prudence Atom diagram. The fuel for values and beliefs is either faith or fear. Faith or fear can define who you are. Like in the story we shared about the two wolves (good and evil) described in Book 2 (Conversation, Conduct, Character, & COVID-19), the wolf who wins is the wolf you choose to feed. Faith is defined in the Bible as "the substance of things hoped for, the evidence of things not seen" (Hebrews 11:1). In psychology, fear is typically defined as emotion which is induced by a perceived threat of someone or something being dangerous (Psychology Blog, 2020).

As the authors of the Prudent Leadership Book Series, we advocate personal freedom and dedicate the writings to all those who value personal freedom. Therefore, to be your authentic self, we encourage living fearlessly by choosing to apply faith according to your values and beliefs and overcome fearful thoughts, emotions, and behaviors. Motivations of fear come from three places of present or past experiences and can be projected into a future state or outcome: (1) Meaningful, (2) Associative, and (3) Active.

The Meaningful place is a need motivated by something (a resource) to be acquired, developed, or retained – as related to Maslow's Hierarchy of

Needs (Maslow 1943; 1954; 1970) and Hobfoll's (2001) Conversation of Resource theories shown in the Nucleus of the Prudence Atom. The Associative place is a need motivated by your relationship with people, organizations, and technology. The Active place is the need motivated to take specific actions and achieve goals – as related to Self-Leadership Theory (Neck & Houghton, 2006).

What do I need now?

Maslow's Hierarchy of Needs Theory

Leader

Values/Beliefs

Conservation of Resources Theory (COR)

Self-Leadership Theory

What personal resources do I want to attract, develop, or retain?

What outcomes do I desire?

Self-Reflection Questions:

Meaningful and Timely – something to be acquired / resource(s)

1. What is your most pressing need right now?

2. What obstacles do you see in the way of getting what you need?

3. How should the obstacles be removed?

4. Who can help you remove the obstacles?

5. What happens if the obstacles are not removed?

6. Should you apply faith or fear to this pressing need?

a. Why? | What do you really believe concerning this pressing need?

b. What justifies your beliefs are true concerning this pressing need?

c. What opposing evidence could invalidate what you believe to be true?

Associative and Healthy: People, Organizations, & Technology

1. Who is in your circle of support?

2. Are the people in your circle of support motivated by faith or fear?

3. Who should stay in your circle of support? | Why?

4. Who should leave your circle of support? | Why?

5. What technology supports getting your needs met in a healthy way?

Active and Prudent: Actions to Achieve Goals

1. What is the specific goal to be achieved?

2. What actions need to be taken? | Put the actions in sequenced order.

How prudent are these actions? | Apply the Prudence Atom concept to assess your values and beliefs and perceived risks for taking these actions.

1. Who am I to apply meaningful and timely acquisition of resources?

2. Who am I to apply associative and healthy relationships?

3. Who am I to apply active and prudent actions to achieve goals?

As you ponder these questions, let us consider a shepherd boy whose own father did not think he was anyone special to be considered a leader, yet alone the next king (1 Samuel 16: 8-11). It is possible David was born illegitimate, because he writes is Psalms 51:5 that he was conceived in sin. When Samuel the prophet came to Jesse to anoint one of his sons to be the next king, Jesse presented seven of his sons to pass before Samuel and only disclosed his other son, David when Samuel pressed the issue about all his sons being present. This biblical story shows the humble beginnings of King David (1040 BC – 970 BC) who tended sheep and fearlessly defended his flock when a lion or bear came to take out a lamb – he would go after it, strike it, and deliver it.

So, when David heard of the Philistine giant, named Goliath, seeking to enslave the Israeli people, the essence of who David was rose up from the inside. David saw the cause for action and while others were fearful of the Philistines and their military might with men of giant stature, David's perspective was different. David asked an audacious question, "Who is this uncircumcised Philistine that he should defy the armies of the living God? (1 Samuel 17:26). David's confidence convinced King Saul to let him proceed in battle against Goliath by his strong conviction of past successes with killing lions and bears to take on the giant. For example, David said to King Saul, "The Lord who delivered me from the paw of the lion and from the paw of the bear, He will deliver me from the hand of this Philistine" (1 Samuel 17:37). Saul then clothed David with his armor, but none of it fit right and it was too heavy.

David went back to who he knew he was, a shepherd boy, who knew how to wield a staff in hand and pick out five smooth stones with his sling in hand to draw near the enemy and take him out (1 Samuel 17:40). Goliath was disdained towards him as he saw a youth, ruddy, and good-looking and started to mock and curse David and his God.

"Am I a dog, that you come to me with sticks? Come to me and I will give your flesh to the birds of the air and the beasts of the field!"

David responded, "you come to me with sword, spear, and javelin, but I come to you in the name of the Lord of hosts, the God of the armies of Israel, whom you have defied. This day the Lord will deliver you into my hand, I will strike you and take your head from you" (1 Samuel 17: 45-46) and the rest is history. Here we have an amazing story showing the power of internal agreement within and with God to apply faith and boldly go do what no one else wanted to do. David's approach was meaningful and with plausible justification to base his capability on past experiences relevant to warfare showing how his ability to take out a lion and bear were transferrable skills to taking out the giant, Goliath.

David's association was healthy to the people, nation, and the God he loved and the technology he used (five smooth stones) was sufficient for the job at hand. David's actions were active and prudent aligning his values and beliefs with his thoughts, emotions, and behaviors to see the perceived risk as faith rather than fear. These key lessons gleaned from the story of David and Goliath show us that when you self-reflect on past situations, you can learn who you are, by what you did, and you can start to manage your life with a business mindset for identifying and procuring resources needed and taking appropriate actions to get them and achieve goals.

Faith and fear are two powerful motivating forces for action. Faith actions propel you to move forward to overcome or achieve something. Fear actions can cause you to freeze in place, run away and hide, or fight because you are backed into a corner without no where else to go. However, there are times and situations where you may feel numb or so overwhelmed that faith and fear become blurred and you need help to move forward. If you feel mentally/emotionally challenged to the point where you cannot move forward or it is too painful to face alone, help is available! Please consider using the resources below.

Mental Health Crisis Resources

The following resources were collectively provided by the Ethan Bean Mental Wellness Foundation (EBMWF) https://ethanbean.org/:

National Alliance on Mental Health (NAMI) offers much support for an immediate or on-going mental health crisis. Please visit https://www.nami.org/Support-Education. Or **tinyurl.com/helpnami**

Text: 741741 This is a crisis hotline that helps provide immediate support to take you from a "hot" situation or feeling to a "cool" one.

National Suicide Prevention Lifeline, **1-800-273-TALK (8255)**

Remember, no matter your situation, there may be someone, right now, available to help you understand your choices (EBMWF, 2020).

5. Manage Your Life Like a Business

National and local governments all have regulations, statues, and laws. Organizations have policies, processes, and procedures. What do individuals have? Should not individuals also have the same? Let us consider what life could look like if you decided to lead yourself like a business with personal policies, procedures, and processes. Using the example of David and Goliath, let us self-reflect on past successes and what was done to achieve outcomes. The Personal Policies template is a tool to develop personal policies, procedures, and processes to facilitate authenticity and make prudent decisions in accordance to who you are. The template is a simple way to organize your thoughts and flesh out the details that matter to you. To use the template, think back to a time when you achieved a personal success, big or small. All that matters is that it was meaningful to you. We include an example to help you get started in this self-reflection process.

In Example #1, the person identifies a past success of overcoming fear of speaking in public. Using that as a foundation for future success, the personal policy to be formalized is enumerated as Policy 1.0 and titled, *Respecting My Voice to Be Heard by Others*. The purpose of this policy is to develop credibility to self and others that their perspective is valid and worthy of being heard. The procedure column represents the what of the policy and the process column represents the how it is to be done. In this example, data handling is the procedure to accompany the personal policy and the process is how the procedure is to be accomplished.

The procedure for data handling involves two areas of using data responsibly and applying critical thinking as a means to instill confidence in self and others that the person's analysis and interpretation is logical and within scope. How this will be accomplished is the process using the

C.R.A.A.P. Model, a framework for ensuring sources of data are current, relevant, have authority, accuracy, and are purposeful to the matter at hand.

In Example #2, referring back to the story of David and Goliath, David could identify his past success of killing the lion and bear to deliver the lambs and sheep from the enemy. He could then develop his first policy (Policy 1.0) as Standing My Ground & Defending My Flock. The purpose of this personal policy would be to maintain sovereignty over all resources within one's individual stewardship. The procedure to stand my ground and defend my flock would include maintaining equipment/technology. In David's case he had a staff, sling shot, smooth stones, and a bag pouch to store his stones. The process of how David implemented his policy was to practice his rock throwing and wielding of staff.

Personal Policies Template / Examples

Past Successes (Foundation)	Policy Topic	Procedure (What)	Process (How)
Example #1: Overcame my fear of speaking in public settings.	Policy 1.0: Respecting my voice to be heard by others Purpose: To develop credibility to self and others that the perspective I share is valid and worthy of being heard.	Data handling: Use data responsibly. Apply critical thinking to instill confidence in self and others that my analysis and interpretation is logical and within scope.	Apply the C.R.A.A.P. Model to data/information: Current Relevant Authority Accurate Purposeful
Example #2: David Stand my ground & defend my flock	Policy 1.0: Stand my ground & defend my flock Purpose: To maintain sovereignty over all resources within my individual stewardship.	Equipment & Technology: Maintain equipment and adequate inventory levels of ammunition.	Practice rock throwing and wielding of staff.
Example #3: Theodore Roosevelt (TR) Strenuous Living	Policy 1.0: Strenuous Life Policy Purpose: Be the best in all things physical.	Exercise: Engage in daily exercise through sports activities (boxing, tennis, hiking, rowing, polo, and horseback riding).	Play hard and achieve personal performance goals.

In Example 3, we could say Theodore Roosevelt had a personal policy called *Strenuous Living*. The purpose of TR's strenuous life policy was to be the best he could be in all things physical. His procedures included boxing, tennis, hiking, rowing, polo, and horseback riding. His processes were playing hard to achieve personal performance goals. We could say Theodore Roosevelt had a personal policy called Strenuous Living. The purpose of TR's strenuous life policy was to be the best he could be in all things physical. His procedures included boxing, tennis, hiking, rowing, polo, and horseback riding. His processes were playing hard to achieve personal performance goals.

What examples can you think of that would make for a meaningful personal policy for yourself?

Use this blank Personal Policies Template to capture and organize your thoughts for developing a meaningful personal policy:

My Personal Policies Template

Past Successes (Foundation)	Policy Topic	Procedure (What)	Process (How)

What do the examples you thought of reveal about who you are?

Like in business, policies are only effective if you implement them. Otherwise, they are just words on paper bound in documents and files. Therefore, develop as many personal policies you feel are necessary to create healthy boundaries and to promote your authenticity. Get comfortable saying no to people and situations that you know are prone to cognitive dissonance (Festinger, 1957) – that uncomfortable feeling inside when you are faced with having to say or do something that does not align with what you know to be true according to your values and beliefs. For example, "No, I am not going to say / do that because it violates my personal policy of doing onto others as I would like them to do on to me."

Other areas for consideration of personal policy include your work/life balance in the context of advancing technology and its influence on artificial intelligence (AI). Additionally, your sense of being in a real world or in a virtual or augmented reality world, dexterity, power, independence and what that means to your social and moral self are the other considerations for personal policy. For example, similar patterns in neural network programming to mimic human neural circuits (brain activity) show how robots are evolving in human likeness to blur the lines of ethics in who's who and the ethical treatment of bio-engineered humanoids – these concepts might sound far-fetched to those not familiar with advancing technology. Nevertheless, now is a good time to familiarize yourself with technological changes and what that means to you for privacy and data protection.

For example, the data brokering industry collects all kinds of information about you and sells it for profit. Information includes your contact information, your purchasing habits, and the data can come from courthouse records, website cookies, voter registration, online surveys, sweepstakes entries, warranty registrations, etc. Machine learning algorithms process high speed data analysis creating digital profiles of you with categorizations to determine who you are. According to Migliore & Chinta (2017), here are some of the labels (red-lining) you could be put into with impact to your credit score, insurance rates, and employment opportunities. These categories include: "Plus-size Apparel, African American Professional, Biker/Hell's Angels, Allergy Sufferer, Exercise –

Sporty Living, Working Class Mom, Burdened by Debt: Singles, X-tra Needy, Credit Crunched: City Families, Ethnic Second-City Stragglers, Fragile Families, and Small Town Shallow Pockets" (p. 50).

How do you feel about being put into one or more of these categories?

The average person is not even aware of the data collection going on every time they use the Internet. Although we are passed the point of no return with machine/deep learning in artificial intelligence (AI) practices, all you can do is be aware that every time you use digital technology, post in social media, or complete online registrations, you are feeding the beast and contributing to the field of data science. Nevertheless, do what you can, with what you have, and where you are at – defend and sustain your right to personal freedom and personal privacy.

Apply Personal Reflection:

1. What does this mean for who I am and my future choices?

2. What can I do now to best prepare with what I have and where I am?

3. What is the right attitude to have towards myself, others, and God?

Listed here also are other areas of application for personal policy development where boundaries may be needed in relationships to guard your inner you and project your best you with parents, co-workers, dating, money, self-care & well-being, etc. Also, because we live in an ambiguous and uncertain world of constant change, it is a good practice to avoid mind traps that protect ego and identity. For example, in our desire to keep things simple, we may be too quick to accept rationalization when we should apply critical thinking and test our assumptions to confirm if they are true. Or, we may go with how we feel. However, if something feels right, it does not always mean it is right – better to think below the surface of feelings.

Most people do not like conflict, so falling into agreement too quickly with others may create a mind trap that blocks prudent decision-making – do not be afraid of conflict. Conflict is good when all parties have opportunity to speak and be heard with dialog focused on the idea or problem and not the person raising the concerns.

Another mind trap is control, because it makes us feel safer if we can steer the ship to reduce risks and avoid problems. However, the reality is we live in an unpredictable world of advancing technology and ongoing change. Therefore, start practicing **the art of feeling comfortable with ambiguity**. We say *art* because you are unique, and your experience and level of comfort will be different from others. By going against your natural inclinations to feel comfortable, you exercise your senses and sharpen your mind to think better and make prudent decisions – a personal attribute of TR living the strenuous life.

6. Summary

Life is a journey; enjoy the experience. Learn to learn and learn to lead self. Understanding is everything. Therefore, get understanding. Take the time needed to reflect what you have learned and how you have grown. Like the beauty of Crater Lake, that Theodore Roosevelt preserved for an infinite number of generations to enjoy, understand that beauty is only skin deep. Do not fall victim to any number of fallacies. For example, *Jumping on the Bandwagon* or *Appealing to a Higher Authority*, believing a certain way because others around you believe that way. Apply diligence to think critically and do your own research. Misguided information can stunt growth, spread fallacies, and lead to prejudice.

In an age of so much fake information, and "alternative facts" it is important to seek out support from reputable sources, accurate and trustworthy, learn to *read between the lines*. Understand the sources from where you obtain information. Be mindful that all information found online and in your social networks, in databases, in libraries, on TV and in podcasts for that matter has some level of bias. Information that comes from educational sources such as schools and religions or from nonprofits, for-profits, government sources, etc., all have missions and purposes. Therefore, it is important to understand the perspective of these organizations, which frames the agenda of their sharing of information.

Become informed and well read. Remember too that haste makes waste, such as fallacies born out of *Hasty Generalizations*. Without critical thinking and proper understanding to apply the right perspective, things designed to help you can look like things designed to destroy you. For example, the surgeon's scalpel is designed to correct and heal the problem. The killer's knife is to destroy. Having good understanding to know the difference between faith and fear is a key to move successfully forward towards achieving your goals.

The thief comes to steal, kill, and destroy, but I [Jesus] have come to give life and life more abundantly – John 10:10

Children are particularly vulnerable to fears, which can reprogram their brains in dysfunctional ways to grow up not knowing who they are and fearfully responding to life like waves tossed in an ocean. Early childhood traumatic events can interfere with neuro pathways in personality development and create disassociate identities and all kinds of psychological disorders. There is no time like now to put safety measures in place to protect children and strengthen the sanctity of body, mind, and spirit.

Whether Gen Z or the youngest of them, called the Alpha generation (in context of tech-savvy children, whose parents are Millennials), they are influencing social-economic changes with their technical dexterity (Pasquarelli & Schultz, 2019). However, we see so many of them struggling with identity, gender, and self-knowing issues. Sheltering in place has helped some feel more comfortable, less exposed to bullying, yet others feel like they are grasping for air and need more freedom like that experienced before the unwelcomed pandemic entered all of our lives.

In the age of COVID-19 where many have been displaced and personal freedom lost, the stability of mental health is being challenged like never before. Let alone any single diagnosis with any number of mental health disorders along the atypical spectrum. The number of atypical students in the U.S. public school system is among the fastest growing population segments (EthanBean.org, 2019). The degree to whether any such disorders can be viewed as a handicap is up to the individual to determine and those mentoring them to support in healthy ways that promote well-being.

Moses led the Jewish people even though he stuttered and so did King George the 6th for that matter lead his people. Your ability to self-lead successfully may be accompanied by a physical or mental challenge, but depending on your values and beliefs, you have the power within to overcome and succeed in the journey of life. For example, it is noble and prudent to be kind and tolerant of self and others. To give self and others the freedom to discover personal identity is prudent.

Who Am I is an open-end question in self-discovery. It does not fall under the guise of a standardized test. Self-discovery can be qualitatively measured in the authenticity inspired by you to self-reflect and apply meaning to life situations and relationships with others.

Therefore, whether it is you or another person, err on the side of mercy and grace rather than judgment. Give yourself and others room for imperfections, because everyone is dealing with something on the inside – hurt, fear, frustration, loss/grief, etc. Babe Ruth did not become a legendary home run hitter overnight. It took years of practice, trials and tribulations and strike outs along the way. It also took Hank Aaron more than 20 years of his own career experience to surpass Ruth's record when Aaron hit number 715 on April 8th, 1974 (History.com, n.d).

But the longer you live, the more likely you will experience loss of someone, something, or some place. The legendary award-winning actress Mary Tyler Moore, who exemplified the independent rights of women everywhere and who struggled with alcoholism, diabetes, and losing her 24-year-old son once said, "Take chances, make mistakes. That's how you grow. Pain nourishes your courage. You have to fail in order to practice being brave" (Schultz, 2017, para 19). We all go through trials and tribulations on life's journey and while the struggles we deal with on the inside may be different, we all need love and understanding from the outside to overcome and be the best version of our authentic selves.

So please join us for our next edition in the 20/20 Prudent Leadership series, Book 4: *Programmed for Excellence*. We will celebrate the graduation of Theodore Roosevelt from Harvard University in 1880. Was he programmed for excellence before he got accepted or did any degree of nepotism or cronyism contribute to his amazing accomplishments? Read Book 4 where we will reinforce other TR fascinating life stories for you to decide. Also, we will provide more tools for you to magnify your strengths and mitigate your weaknesses to be who you want to be.

References

Acocella, N. (2020). Moe Berg: Catcher and spy. *EPSN*. Retrieved from http://www.espn.com/classic/biography/s/Berg_Moe.html

Allouche, P. (2018). Who Am I — Judaism's definition of the self. *The Jewish News, Greater Phoenix, Northern Arizona*. Retrieved from http://www.jewishaz.com/religiouslife/who-am-i-judaism-s-definition-of-the-self/article_acb10e1a-f62b-11e7-ab40-83060412f748.html

Barclay, S. (2011). Anneliese Michel exorcism and death. *Historic Mysteries*. Retrieved from https://www.historicmysteries.com/anneliese-michel-exorcism/

Caligor, E., & Stern, B.L. (2020). Diagnosis, Classification, and Assessment of Narcissistic Personality Disorder Within the Framework of Object Relations Theory. Journal of Personality Disorders, 34, 104-121. https://doi.org/10.1521/pedi.2020.34.supp.104

Chong, S. (2004). Life's Big Question: Who Am I? Retrieved from https://www.cardus.ca/comment/article/lifes-big-questions-who-am-i/

CIA (2013). News & information: "Moe" Berg: Sportsman, Scholar, Spy. *Central Intelligence Agency*. Retrieved from https://www.cia.gov/news-information/featured-story-archive/2013-featured-story-archive/moe-berg.html

Cleveland Clinic (2020). Temporal Lobe Seizures. *Cleveland Clinic*. Retrieved from https://my.clevelandclinic.org/health/diseases/17778-temporal-lobe-seizures

EBMWF. (2020). Resources. Retrieved from https://ethanbean.org/emergency%3F

Encyclopedia of Philosophy, (2020). Epistemology. Retrieved from https://plato.stanford.edu/entries/epistemology/

Engineering Insider (2018, April 19). What is triple point? *Engineering Insider*. Retrieved from https://engineeringinsider.org/triple-point/

EthanBean.org. (2019). New children's book for a struggling mental health era. Retrieved from https://ethanbean.org/new-childrens-book-1.

Exorcism of Emily Rose (2005). Retrieved at https://www.imdb.com/title/tt0404032/

Festinger, L. (1957). *A Theory of Cognitive Dissonance.* Stanford, CA: Stanford University Press

Front of the class (2008). Retrieved at https://www.imdb.com/title/tt1292594/

Grange, K. (2011). The old man of the lake. *National Parks Conservation Association*. Retrieved from https://www.npca.org/articles/1016-the-old-man-of-the-lake

History.com. (n.d.). Hank Aaron breaks Babe Ruth's all-time home run record. Retrieved on https://www.history.com/this-day-in-history/aaron-sets-new-home-run-record

Hobfoll, S.E. (2001). The influence of culture, community, and the nested-self in the stress process: Advancing the Conservation of Resources Theory. Applied Psychology: An International Review *50*(3), 337-421.

Korzekwa, M.I., Dell, P.F., Links, P.S., Thabane, L., & Fougere, P. (2009). Dissociation in borderline personality disorder: a detailed look. Journal of Trauma & Dissociation: The Official Journal of the International Society for the Study of Dissociation (ISSD), *10*(3), 346-367. https://doi.org/10.1080/15299730902956838

Laddis, A., Dell, P.F., & Korzekwa, M. (2017). Comparing the symptoms and mechanisms of "dissociation" in dissociative identify disorder and borderline personality disorder. *Journal of Trauma & Dissociation: The Official Journal of the International Society for the Study of Dissociation* (ISSD), *18*(2), 139-173. https://doi.org/10.1080/15299732.2016.1194358.

Lindell, M. (2019). *What are the odds? From crack addict to CEO.* Lindell Publishing: USA.

Maslow, A. H. (1943). A Theory of Human Motivation. *Psychological Review, 50(4)*, 370-96.

Maslow, A. H. (1954). *Motivation and personality*. New York: Harper and Row.

Maslow, A. H. (1970). Motivation and personality. (2nd ed). New York: Harper and Row.

Migliore, L.A. and Chinta, R. (2017). Demystifying the Big Data phenomena for strategic leadership. *SAM Advanced Management Journal, Winter 2017, 82*(1), 48-58.

Neck, C.P. and Houghton, J.D. (2006) Two decades of self-leadership theory and research: Past developments, present trends, and future possibilities. Journal of Managerial Psychology *21*(4), 270–295.

NPS (2020). Crater Lake. *National Park Service* Retrieved from https://www.nps.gov/crla/index.htm

Paoletti, G. (2017). Anneliese Michel and the shocking images from the exorcism of the real Emily Rose. *ATI.* Retrieved from https://allthatsinteresting.com/anneliese-michel-exorcism

Pasquarelli, A. & Schultz, E.J. (2019). Move over Gen Z, Generation Alpha is the one to watch. Retrieved from https://adage.com/article/cmo-strategy/move-gen-z-generation-alpha-watch/316314

Psychology Blog (2020, April 19). *Psychology of fear – definition and introduction.* Retrieved from https://www.whatpsychologyis.com/psychology-of-fear/

SABR (2020). Babe Ruth, Brooklyn Dodgers Coach. Society for American Baseball Research. Retrieved from https://sabr.org/research/babe-ruth-brooklyn-dodgers-coach

Schultz, B. (2017). Mary Tyler Moore's greatest quotes. Retrieved from https://www.entrepreneur.com/article/288331

Schwartz, L. (n.d.). Lovable Ruth was everyone's Babe. Retrieved from http://www.espn.com/classic/biography/s/ruth_babe.html
Standard Encyclopedia of Philosophy, (2020). Epistemology. Retrieved from https://plato.stanford.edu/entries/epistemology/

Time Magazine (1976, Sept 6). A phenomenon of fear. *Time Magazine 108(10)*, 68.

Tourette Association of America (n.d). *What is Tourette?* Retrieved at: https://tourette.org/about-tourette/overview/what-is-tourette/

Voice of Unity. (2015). Who Am I. Retrieved from https://www.ius.org.uk/who-am-i/

WebMD (2020). Dissociative Identity Disorder (Multiple Personality Disorder). *WebMD.* Retrieved at https://www.webmd.com/mental-health/dissociative-identity-disorder-multiple-personality-disorder#1

Glossary

Algorithm: Programmed function(s) applied to a data set.

Atypical: Individual for whom according to the American Psychiatric Association DSM-V has a behavior or mental challenge for which there is no formal diagnosis. It may include any number of autistic behaviors.

Beliefs: Personal truth to make meaning of life experiences; firmly held opinions or convictions that something does or does not exist.

Cognitive Consonance: Lack of cognitive dissonance; no conflicting situation of action or ideas that clash with personal sense of right and wrong.

Cognitive Dissonance: Uncomfortable feeling (mental or emotional stress) when a presenting situation of actions or ideas do not agree with personal sense of right and wrong.

Conservation of Resources (COR) Theory: The stress response a person experiences when they perceive resources are threatened or are at risk of being depleted or destroyed; the response is to protect and mitigate risk.

Dissociative Identity Disorder (DID): A severe form of dissociation in the mental process of a person's thoughts, emotions, memories, behaviors, and overall identify of who one is. The process of dissociation can create multiple personalities or a split within one identity of self.

Epistemology: The study of knowledge, justification, and rationality of belief.

Faith: The substance of things hoped for, the evidence of things not seen.

Fear: An emotion which is induced by a perceived threat of someone or something being dangerous.

Machine Learning: Applications within artificial intelligence (AI) systems designed to learn automatically via a synthesis of algorithms to improve recognition and responses.

Maslow's Hierarchy of Needs Theory: Widely accepted as a common-sense approach to understanding human motivations of physical and psychological needs in the order of importance.

Mental Health: The current condition of individual involving his or her psychological and emotional well-being.

Neurodiversity: Or neurodiverse, are individuals who display any number of autism behaviors and/or one who may have normal variations of brain function. Sometimes used as a synonym for atypical.

Personal Epistemology: Deep self-reflection in study of self, knowledge of what is known and its justification, and rationality of belief – one's own personal truth.

Prudence: Discipline of self-leadership and personal governance to apply practical reasoning in decision-making motivated by truth to do good.

Prudent Adam: Character depiction of a human being, who consistently practices prudent leadership.

Prudence Atom: Analogy that uses an atomic-level perspective to explain the internal interactions of values and beliefs (nucleus) with thoughts, emotions, and behaviors (electrons) during situations of perceived risk.

Prudent Decision-Making: Intentional application of the discipline of self-leadership and personal governance to apply practical reasoning in decision-making motivated by truth to do good.

Prudent Leadership: The intentional leading of self (self-leadership) in mindful personal governance to regulate behaviors, lifestyle, and make prudent decisions that are motivated by truth to do good in goal achievement and influence others to do the same.

Self-leadership theory: Personal governance of thoughts, communications, emotions, and behaviors in the overall management of self to pursue/achieve goals.

Sublimation: A process of the *Triple Point* phenomenon occurring when there is an intersection of equal temperature and pressure at all three phases to transition a physical change of state from solid to gas, bypassing the liquid state.

Tourette Syndrome: A Tic Disorder expressed involuntary with repetitive movements and vocalizations.

Triple Point: Phenomenon of thermodynamics that occurs when a substance has temperature and pressure equal at each of the three phases: gas, liquid, and solid.

Values: Strongly held beliefs about what is important, acceptable, and appreciated.

ABOUT THE AUTHORS

LauraAnn Migliore, Ph.D.

Dr. Migliore is an experienced leader, innovative researcher, and inspiring educator, specializing in organizational strategy and the psychology of learning for employee training and leadership development programs through the lens of digital technology and the Internet of Things (IoT) - Big Data, Machine Learning, and 3D Virtual Learning. LauraAnn's professional background includes over 30-years diverse work experiences in the automotive industry, higher education, consulting, healthcare, and non-profit. She is published in the areas of personality and cross-cultural research, leadership, corporate governance, and mobile technology. Migliore is an Organizational Strategist at Abundant Knowledge, L.L.C. and 2020 President of the Association for Talent Development (ATD) Southwest Florida Chapter.

Erik Bean, Ed.D.

Dr. Bean serves both industry and academia. He is an engagement expert and a recognized thought leader in strategic customer experience communication. As a scholar, Erik holds a doctorate in education with sanctioned research interests in cultural competence, leadership, immediacy, meditation, and mental health. He is the section editor of Leadership Perspectives, *The Journal of Leadership Studies*, John Wiley & Sons. He also is executor of the Ethan Bean Mental Wellness Foundation, EthanBean.org, a Michigan 501(c)3 public charity and is co-author of *Ethan's Healthy Mind Express: A Children's First Mental Health Primer* book.

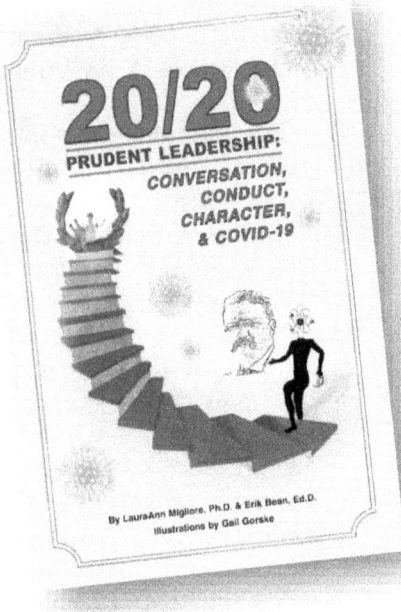

pandemic. He would continue to live by his own indelible words, "Do what you can, with what you have, where you are at." Now let us pause for a reinvigorating look at The Three Cs plus one. For TR would agree while health is the new wealth, prudence is the currency of choice we can all bank on! **ISBN: 978-1-7347801-1-6**

EACH RELEASE DATE CORRESPONDS TO THEODORE ROOSEVELT'S UNPRECEDENTED ACCOMPLISHMENTS:

1898 TR appointed lieutenant colonel of **First U.S. Volunteer Cavalry Regiment** – aka "**ROUGH RIDERS**"

www.ingramcontent.com/pod-product-compliance
Lightning Source LLC
Chambersburg PA
CBHW071642050426
42443CB00026B/944